ALSO BY EVE ENSLER

The Vagina Monologues

Necessary Targets: A Story of Women and War

THE
GOOD
BODY

EVE

ENSLER

VILLARD • NEW YORK

THE

GOOD

BODY

Published in the United States by Villard Books, an imprint of
The Random House Publishing Group, a division of
Random House, Inc., New York.

VILLARD BOOKS and "V" CIRCLED Design are registered
trademarks of Random House, Inc.

Library of Congress Cataloging-in-Publication Data
Ensler, Eve.
The good body / Eve Ensler.
p.   cm.
ISBN 0-375-50284-X
1. Women—Drama.   2. Body image—Drama.
3. Body, Human—Drama.   I. Title.
PS3555.N75G66 2004
812'.54—dc22   2004057592

Printed in the United States of America on acid-free paper

Villard Books website address: www.villard.com

2 4 6 8 9 7 5 3 1

First Edition

For Colette,

that she may

choose to be great

instead of good;

for Ariel,

who loves my belly;

and

for my mother

Preface

In the midst of a war in Iraq, in a time of escalating global terrorism, when civil liberties are disappearing as fast as the ozone layer, when one out of three women in the world will be beaten or raped in her lifetime, why write a play about my stomach?

Maybe because my stomach is one thing I feel I have control over, or maybe because I have hoped that my stomach is something I could get control over. Maybe because I see how my stomach has come to occupy my attention, I see how other women's stomachs or butts or thighs or hair or skin have come to occupy their attention, so that we have very little left for the war in Iraq—or much else, for that matter. When a group of ethnically diverse, economically disadvantaged women in the United States was recently asked about the one thing they would change in their lives if they could, the majority of these women said they would lose weight. Maybe I identify with these women because I have bought into the idea that if my stomach were flat, then I would be good, and I would be safe. I would be protected. I would be accepted, admired, important, loved. Maybe because for most of my life I have felt wrong, dirty, guilty, and bad, and my stomach is the carrier, the pouch for all that self-hatred. Maybe because my stomach has become the repository for my sorrow, my childhood scars, my unfulfilled ambition, my unexpressed rage. Like a toxic dump, it is where the explosive trajectories collide—the Judeo-Christian imperative to be good; the patriarchal mandate that women be quiet, be less; the consumer-state imperative to be better, which is based on the assumption that you are born wrong and bad, and that being better always involves spending money, lots of money. Maybe because, as the world rapidly divides into fundamentalist camps, reductive sound bites, and polarizing platitudes, an exploration of my stomach and the life therein has the potential to shatter these dangerous constraints.

This journey has been different from the one I undertook in *The Vagina Monologues*. I was worried about vaginas when I began that play. I was worried about the shame associated with vaginas and I was worried about what was happening to vaginas, in the dark. As I talked about vaginas and to vaginas, I became even more worried about the onslaught of violence done to women and their vaginas around the world.

There was, of course, the great celebration of vaginas as well. Pleasure, discovery, sex, moans, power. I suppose I had this fantasy that after finally coming home into my vagina, I could relax, get on with life. This was not the case. The deadly self-hatred simply moved into another part of my body.

The Good Body began with me and my particular obsession with my "imperfect" stomach. I have charted this self-hatred, recorded it, tried to follow it back to its source. Here, unlike the women in *The Vagina Monologues*, I am my own victim, my own perpetrator. Of course, the tools of my self-victimization have been made readily available. The pattern of the perfect body has been programmed into me since birth. But whatever the cultural influences and pressures, my preoccupation with my flab, my constant dieting, exercising, worrying, is self-imposed. *I* pick up the magazines. *I* buy into the ideal. *I* believe that blond, flat girls have the secret. What is far more frightening than narcissism is the zeal for self-mutilation that is spreading, infecting the world.

I have been to more than forty countries in the last six years. I have seen the rampant and insidious poisoning: skin-lightening creams sell as fast as toothpaste in Africa and Asia; the mothers of eight-year-olds in America remove their daughters' ribs so they will not have to worry about dieting; five-year-olds in Manhattan do strict asanas so they won't embarrass their parents in public by being chubby; girls vomit and starve themselves in China and Fiji and everywhere; Korean women remove Asia from their eyelids . . . the list goes on and on.

I have been in a dialogue with my stomach for the past three years. I have entered my belly—the dark wet underworld—to get at the secrets there. I have talked with women in surgical centers in Beverly Hills; on the sensual beaches of Rio de Janeiro; in the gyms of Mumbai, New York, Moscow; in the hectic and crowded beauty salons of Istanbul, South Africa, and Rome. Except for a rare few, the women I met loathed at least one part of their body. There was almost always one part that they longed to change, that they had a medicine cabinet full of products devoted to transforming or hiding or reducing or straightening or lightening. Just about every woman believed that if she could just get that part right, everything else would work out. Of course, it is an endless heartbreaking campaign.

Some of the monologues in *The Good Body* are based on well-known women like Helen Gurley Brown and Isabella Rossellini. Those monologues, which grew out of a series of conversations with each of these fascinating women, are not recorded interviews, but interpretations of the lives they offered me. Some of the other characters are based on real lives, real stories. Many are invented.

This play is my prayer, my attempt to analyze the mechanisms of our imprisonment, to break free so that we may spend more time running the world than running away from it; so that we may be consumed by the sorrow of the world rather than consuming to avoid that sorrow and suffering. This play is an expression of my hope, my desire, that we will all refuse to be Barbie, that we will say no to the loss of the particular, whether it be to a voluptuous woman in a silk sari, or a woman with defining lines of character in her face, or a distinguishing nose, or olive-toned skin, or wild curly hair.

I am stepping off the capitalist treadmill. I am going to take a deep breath and find a way to survive not being flat or perfect. I am inviting you to join me, to stop trying to be anything, anyone other than who you are. I was moved by women in Africa who lived close to the earth and didn't understand what it meant to not love their body. I was lifted by older women in India who celebrated their roundness. I was inspired by Marion Woodman, a great Jungian analyst, who gave me confidence to trust what I know. She has said that "instead of transcending ourselves, we must move into ourselves."

Tell the image makers and magazine sellers and the plastic surgeons that you are not afraid. That what you fear the most is the death of imagination and originality and metaphor and passion. Then be bold and LOVE YOUR BODY. STOP FIXING IT. It was never broken.

THE

GOOD

BODY

When I was a little girl people used to ask me, What do you want to be when you grow up? Good, I would say. I want to be good. Becoming good was harder than becoming a doctor or an astronaut or a lifeguard. There are tests to pass to become those things—you have to learn dissection or conquer gravity or practice treading water. Becoming good was not like that. It was abstract. It felt completely out of reach. It became the only thing that mattered to me. If I could be good, everything would be all right. I would fit in. I would be popular. I would skip death and go straight to heaven. If you asked me now what this means, to be good, I still don't know exactly. When I was growing up in the fifties, "good" was simply what girls were supposed to be. They were good. They were pretty, perky. They had a blond Clairol wave in their hair. They wore girdles and waist cinchers and pumps. They got married. They looked married. They waited to be given permission. They kept their legs together, even during sex.

In recent years, good girls join the Army. They climb the corporate ladder. They go to the gym. They accessorize. They wear pointy, painful shoes. They wear lipstick if they're lesbians; they wear lipstick if they're not. They don't eat too much. They don't eat at all. They stay perfect. They stay thin.

I could never be good. This feeling of badness lives in every part of my being. Call it anxiety or despair. Call it guilt or shame. It occupies me everywhere. The older, seemingly clearer and wiser I get, the more devious, globalized, and terrorist the badness becomes. I think for many of us—well, for most of us—well, maybe for all of us—there is one particular part of our body where the badness manifests itself, our thighs, our butt, our breasts, our hair, our nose, our little toe. You know what I'm talking about? It doesn't matter where I've been in the world, whether it's Tehran where women are—smashing and remodeling their noses to looks less Iranian, or in Beijing where they are breaking their legs and adding bone to be taller, or in Dallas where they are surgically whittling their feet in order to fit into Manolo Blahniks or Jimmy Choos. Everywhere, the women I meet generally hate one particular part of their bodies. They spend most of their lives fixing it, shrinking it. They have medicine cabinets with products devoted to transforming it. They have closets full of clothes that cover or enhance it. It's as if they've been given their own little country called their body, which they get to tyrannize, clean up, or control while they lose all sight of the world.

What I can't believe is that someone like me, a radical feminist for nearly thirty years, could spend this much time thinking about my stomach. It has become my tormentor, my distractor; it's my most serious committed relationship. It has protruded through my clothes, my confidence, and my ability to work. I've tried to sedate it, educate it, embrace it, and most of all, erase it.

.

My body will be mine when I'm thin. I will eat a little at a time, small bites. I will vanquish ice cream. I will purge with green juices. I will see chocolate as poison and pasta as a form of self-punishment. I will work not to feel full again. Always moving toward full, approaching full but never really full. I will embrace my emptiness, I will ride it into holy zones. Let me be hungry. Let me starve. Please.

———————

Bread is Satan. I stop eating bread. This is the same as not eating food. Four days in, a scrawny actress friend tells me, "Eve, your stomach has nothing to do with diet." What? "It's the change of life," she says. "All you need is some testosterone." I try to imagine what I would be like, totally bread deprived and shot up with testosterone. "Serial killer" comes to mind.

I realize at night that I am grinding my jaw. It's my hunger for bread. The closest I let myself come is dried bread—pretzels, flatbread, bread sticks. These are the memory of bread, the freeze-dried, sound-bite version of bread. It's crispy. It keeps cracking, particularly pretzels, thousands of pieces breaking inside your mouth. It's a lot to think about, so why the fuck am I still thinking about bread?

I watch Ab Roller infomercials until four A.M. as I eat a bag—no, a family-size bag—of peanut M&M's. I try to buy an Ab Roller by phone but they're really hostile on the 800-"Roll-It-Away" number. They're probably starving, too. They interviewed all these once famous blond women to see if they had better results with the Ab Roller than with sit-ups, crunches, or curls. Of course all of them said yes. All of them were flat flat flat. The next day I bite the bullet, well, at least I bite something, and hire Vernon, a fascistic trainer. Of course, he's totally flat and muscular. He looks at me with pity and punishment. Right away he has me lifting heavy objects. Very heavy. The good news is I'm so fucking sore I can't move my head so I'm unable to see my disgusting stomach anymore.

I'm walking—actually, I'm limping—down a New York City street, and I catch a glimpse of this blond, pointy-breasted, raisin-a-day-stomached smiling girl on the cover of Cosmo magazine. She is there every minute, somewhere in the world, smiling down on me, on all of us. She's omnipresent. She's the American Dream, my personal nightmare. Pumped straight from the publishing power plant into the bloodstream of our *culture and neurosis. She is multiplying on every cover. She was passed through my mother's milk and so I don't even know that I'm contaminated. I just want to be like her. I want to be Barbie. And it doesn't matter that if I were anatomically structured like Barbie I would be unable to walk and would be forced to crawl on all fours. Don't get me wrong, I'm my own perpetrator, I'm my own victim. I pick up the magazines. No, no, no. It's the* possibility *of being skinny good that keeps me buying. Oh, God, I discover a Starbucks maple walnut scone expanding in me, creeping out. Flabby age leaking through the cracks. Big Macs, French fries, Pizza Land, four helpings, can't stop. My stomach is chicken wings, dipping butter, fried shrimp, fried zucchini, fried ice cream, fried dumplings, fried anything, fried right. My stomach is America. I want to drown in the cement. There's obviously something I'm just not getting. I am going to go and find the woman who thought this up. Maybe if I listen carefully, she'll reveal the secret.*

Helen Gurley Brown

AUTHOR AND PIONEERING EDITOR OF

COSMOPOLITAN MAGAZINE

(*Doing sit-ups*) . . . seven, eight, nine—Eve dear, come in, pussycat. . . . ninety-nine, one hundred. (*Stops sit-ups*) I'm multitasking. I do ten sit-ups for every shot. Do you like her? (*Referring to slides*) She's the December cover—we're going rounder for the Christmas season. We're desperate for the feeling of holiday fullness and cheer.

Eighty years old, one hundred sit-ups twice a day,

I'm down to ninety pounds. Another ten years, I'll be down to nothing. But even then I won't feel beautiful. I accept this terrible condition. It's driven me to be disciplined and successful.

Through *Cosmo* I've been able to help women everywhere.

I've been able to help everyone but me. Ironic. Come on in, Eve, let's get cozy. Help yourself to some pumpkin seeds, dear, they're toasted. Energy. That's the closest I ever come to cooking. I never did get the nurture gene.

My mother never saw me. She saw acne. She took me to the doctor twice a week for five years. He opened, postuled, and squeezed my face. He left it battered. He would keep an X-ray machine on my face, five minutes at a time. This was long before we knew about X rays. He burned the bottom layer off my face. After the appointments we would drive around, my mother and I. She would cry, I would cry. "How can I be a happy person, Helen?" she would say. "Your sister is in a wheelchair with polio. Your father is dead. And you, Helen, you have acne."

When I was ten, my friend Elizabeth was swinging from the tree. She fell and everyone came and made a huge fuss over her. I told this to my mother and she said, "Of course: Elizabeth's pretty. People make a fuss over girls who are pretty. That's why you, you will need brains."

(*Doing sit-ups again*) Don't get things fixed, Eve. Don't do it. (*Stops sit-ups*) If you do, another thing always breaks down. I had my eyes done when I was forty. I thought that would do. But no. Tried it again when I was fifty-six. First full face-lift at sixty-three. Second at sixty-seven. Third at seventy-three. I'm desperate for another, but there's no skin left on my face. Yesterday they took some fat out of my backside and they shot it into my cheeks. I think even you would approve, Eve. I am recycling. My shrink thinks I'm still doing this for my mother, Cleo's gone almost twenty years. Can you imagine, I'm still doing this for her? I never had a daughter. But if I did have a daughter, I would tell her she was beautiful and lovely every minute. If she asked, "Helen"—oh God, she wouldn't say Helen, she's not my assistant.

If she said, "Mother, am I as pretty as Brooke Shields?" I'd have to do a little hedging. "You're not classic," I'd say. "But you're beautiful in your way, dear." Eve, I would really have to practice this. One thing I never had to practice was sex. I took to it like a duck to water. It's been a good week. My husband and I had sex two days in a row. Not bad for eighty. My husband, he's feisty, always has been. The crazy thing is he's always thought I was beautiful, but of course that doesn't count, I mean, he loves me. (*Suddenly snapping her fingers, moving things along*) Enzio, it's Christmas, but this isn't charity. Move it along. I'm ready for the Mrs. Santa thong shot.

Thanks for sharing. . . . I'm so depressed. In Helen's world, Mrs. Santa lives in Iceland and she's wearing a thong and I bet she looks hot in it. Even Rudolph probably has a hard-on. In Eve's world, I run into a friend on the street. She's strangely enthusiastic, pointing at my stomach.

"Eve, congratulations! For you, I bet it's a little warrior girl."

Eve on treadmill

I go straight to the gym.

I do not pass Starbucks, I do not pass

Häagen-Dazs.

I strap myself to the treadmill.

Four hours, six hours. People are pissed off. I

don't care.

I am working on an abortion.

A girl's got a right to choose.

I have rubber burns on my sneakers

I smell like a traffic accident

Big surprise: Vernon says, "Great! Keep
    going."

Eve doing sit-ups

A hundred and twenty sit-ups twice a day.

I feel like a Marine.

Arms up in air

"Pain is weakness leaving the body."

"Pain is weakness leaving the body."

Activity disorder. Exercise bulimia.

I think I've got it.

Would you still power-walk in a sleet storm?
    Uh-huh. Check.

Would you do sit-ups the day after a tummy
    tuck? Uh-huh. Check.

I feel like shit. How do people do this? Why

    do people do this? How does Helen do it?

She's eighty. She's insane.

I need something kinder, I need something gentler; let's face it, I need something easier. Six weeks, I'm already tired of taking care of my body. I need someone else to do it. I'll hire a team. I'll go to a health retreat, a spa. They'll seaweed-wrap it out of me. Exfoliate me. I'm there.

Bernice

AN AFRICAN AMERICAN TEENAGE CAMPER

Call it what it is, Eve, this ain't no spa. This is fat camp. You're here. You're fucked. You better suck it in. I don't know about you but I'm starving. Where are the Cheetos?

They busted a girl in my bunk last night. She had hoarded hundreds of packs of contraband gum, stuffed in the ripped-off head of her little teddy bear. She tried to smush it back together but she had already broken its neck. Fool, she deserves to be starving.

The big question is, Who let the skinny girls in? Skinny bitches don't belong in this camp. They make the rest of us look fat. Skinny bitches drive me nuts. (*Looks down at lunch*) You don't mean to call this lunch.

Skinny bitches don't deserve to be thin. They have no personality. They're just Skinny Bitches. They 're always trying to make us feel sorry for them when their entire torso could fit up my sleeve.

(*Imitates a skinny bitch*) "Oh, look, does this make me look fat? Focus. Focus. Right here. Please look, be honest."

I wanna choke their skinny necks. They 're complaining about their six-pack when I'm carrying a keg.

Fat is as low, disgusting, as gross as you can get. Like when I'm shopping in the regular stores they always keep the plus sizes in the back like porn. I feel like a ho trying things on and the PLUS SIZE sign is always so huge. Just 'cause I'm fat doesn't mean I'm blind. "Excuse me, are you going to eat that? 'Cause if not, can you give it to me? Oh . . . She's saving it for later."

Skinny bitches never have to beg, they never have to work at anything. They're skinny. Fat girls do everything double. We have to be funny. Fat girls give the best head. Don't we, Eve? We work harder to keep our men. Fat girls always swallow.

You know, Eve, last night, after the counselors went to sleep, some of us fat girls, we had a wicked night. We stripped off our bathing suits and we went chunky-dunking in the pool. We jumped off the high diving board and made huge waves. Some of the beach chairs just floated away. It felt so good. We did some fat-girl water ballet. Some Swan Ass Lake. We were pointing our chubby toes and kicking our legs. We look so much better naked than in those made-for-skinny-bitches bathing suits. I have to tell you, in the moonlight we were all round and moundy. We looked beautiful. (*Beat*) Now the skinny bitches are back at lunch huddled around their spoonful of nonfat yogurt and half a nut. I don't know why I'm fat, Eve. I just am. I am fat, I like food. The way it tastes. The way it goes down. I eat for happiness. I love buffets. We eat at home. Oh, we eat. (*Beat*) I never missed my mom so much. I don't look fat when I'm with my mom. My family, we are big people, I do not know why they're trying to get me to act small. They're worried. All this talk from the government about blowing up from obesity. I think this government should be worried about blowing up from all these bombs. I'm starving. Give me my momma's home cooking and her fluffy duck ass, and Supersize it. Fat girls are good people. Aren't we, Eve? We deserve to be skinny bitches.

I get booted out of fat camp for sharing my Zone bars with Bernice, who according to the fat camp police is a minor and not allowed to make nutritional choices. I envy Bernice. She's relaxed. She can openly express her hunger and her anger, and her parents still love her. She loves food. She loves her bread.

My father hated bread. He said only pigs eat bread, only pigs fill up on bread. To eat bread was to reveal your hunger. In his world, to show hunger was gauche, revealing your lack of class and manners. I watched my father pretend to eat night after night and I never sensed that he was interested in food at all. He rearranged his food, then rested his fork between each tiny bite, rested it for a long, long time, time for the food to grow cold or become something else, which food will do if you wait too long. Which is how young girls starve. I know firsthand. I became afraid of food. I had my father's contempt for it. When I was seventeen, my doctor threatened to sue me for malpractice to my own body. Food connected you to life, but, more important, it connected you to people. My father did not like people, and particularly little people, children. He did not like their noise or questions. If I could have starved and lived, I would have. So of course every man I have ever loved loves bread. Needs bread. Brings it home like a hat. Like a newspaper. Brings it home because without it, there is no home. Every man I have ever loved waits at first, seeing that I never remember bread, that for all intents and purposes I do everything I can to avoid bread, the bread becomes what they do. My partner loves pita. He warms them on the gas flame, flipping them over quickly so his hands never burn. Our house always smells like fire, and although the smell makes me deeply sad, it . . . comforts me, too.

My partner loves to eat. Eat right away. Eat everything. Eat without stopping. If he uses his fork it's accidental. He cooks. Well, he makes art with food. It's as much about the color as it is about the garlic. The reds and yellows and greens. He seduced me with his dazzling eggplant salad. He seduced me into swallowing beauty. He seduced me into living. We always share the same plate, so I am less afraid and lonely. We eat fast and put our olive pits on the table. Olives annoyed my father, too. Pits were evidence of eating. My partner will sometimes leave up to fourteen olive pits, and although I could feel some shame (I am my father's daughter), I wished my father had been exposed to these remnants. They would have shocked and revolted him and this would have secretly pleased me.

My father looked like Cary Grant. My mother looked like Doris Day. I was a dead ringer for Anne

Frank. My mother never raised her voice. I tried un-successfully not to make noise in the attic. She was blond and glowed. In her pack of golden puppies I was dark and hairy. Eew! Eew! How did this one get into my litter. My mother would do anything, everything to clean me up, shut me up, make me good, make me right.

When I was eight, I began ballroom dancing les-sons with white gloves. Every Friday night, for six years. I sweated more than the terrified boys and could never learn to let them lead. Then there's the matter of enemas and perms.

My mother cleaned one end and curled the other. When I spoke out, I expressed my unhappiness. Then I was Sarah Bernhardt. I had no idea who Sarah was, but I was sure she was Jewish and in deep shit.

In my Weight Watchers group, after the trauma of the weekly weigh-in, an older Jewish woman from Queens realizes she is eight pounds from her target weight. She is on a pomegranate seed diet. I'm starting it next week. She looks in the mirror and begins weeping. "Oh my God, I look like Selma." I say, "Selma?" She says, "My mother. I look like my mother. I've got my mother's tuches." Then this skinny bitch, Carmen, who never moves, never eats, never shares, suddenly speaks:

Carmen

I know, Mrs. Schwartz, I know. You better be careful.
Strange things can happen. People can take up resi-
dency in your body parts. Maybe it's their way of getting close to you when you can't connect in real life.
Maybe they, like, slow-poison you. What I still don't
get is if they invade you or they're invited.

Now, Puerto Ricans, we're not like the Jews. We
love a big butt. It's the spread we dread. If you get
the spread, you're dead. It's not chicken livers, Mrs.

Schwartz, you can't put it on crackers. It's not an STD. You can take drugs for that before it gets your brain. But the spread, once it begins, makes you completely fucking insane. Good butts, good asses, ooh they are different, they are everything. You want to stick it out, make it visible everywhere you go, particularly on the street, "Hi, baby." We begin practicing when we're young, like driving lessons, backing them up, turning them around, shining them up (tss!) for display. You want them round, plumpy, and high. If I had Janet Jackson's ass, I'd walk backwards.

But the spread is like a lower butt, a second pair of thighs. It's something that oozes out of you. Against your will. It's where you lose your life. When men see the spread, they see their mothers. They see rice and beans and a pissed-off wife with screaming kids in front of a loud half-paid-for TV set.

You have to work really hard to contain the spread after you give birth. Like an oil spill. If you don't stop it right away, it will contaminate everything. Suffocate all the flora and fauna. My mother, wicked queen, she had eight kids, never spread an inch. "Mirror, Mirror, on the wall, who's the most beautiful and paranoid of all? My mother." Latina *Cosmo* girl. She was totally beautiful, real pretty brown, perfect tits, Mercedes-Benz ass. I was the ugly one—or so she said, over and over. When I was a kid she would back me into the mirror at home like a broken-down truck and she would poke at my spread like it was a jellyfish. "Oh, God, Carmen, Carmen, you've got the spread. *Mira. Mira.* It's bad. It's bad, Carmen. You better work hard on a nice waist and a brain or no one will ever fuck you."

I always wore baggy pants and spread covers. That's what we called them. I practiced sitting on a toilet to see what I looked like sitting on a man. It's bad. You can't suck in your spread. It's not like your stomach, Eve. No. So I learned the anti-spread positions. Certain positions that if you stayed real still or kept on a certain angle the spread would not be revealed. It was all about keeping the spread in the shadows. There was one particular trick, I'll show it to you, scooch down, scooch down, all of you. It's called the Spread Tuck. You lift and tuck, lift and tuck. You gotta hold real still, though, or it'll roll right out. I did the Spread Tuck the first time I was going to have intercourse. The sex was going pretty well—I couldn't move, but it was okay. Then the guy got really passionate and shit and grabbed my spread. I screamed. He thought I was losing my virginity, but he had grabbed my spread and it was oozing in his hand. Shit, now he would leave me like my mother said. My mother got the men. I didn't. But she got sick, she got AIDS. She began to fall away. I spread more and more as she disappeared. I spread and spread. I was too humiliated to go out. Then my mother died. At first, I felt nothing. Then, when I was driving away from her funeral in Brooklyn, I don't know why but I started to scream and scream and scream like I was screaming for my life. All those years I just wanted to be pretty and good so you would love me, Mommy. Why didn't you ever see me? Now you're gone. I rode my bike seven hours every day and I cried and cried. I went in the pool and I let my hair be wild. I didn't blow it dry or make it right. I stopped wearing makeup and I didn't diet or even care. Suddenly, this weird shit started happening. It was like I was in this crazy body twilight zone. My spread began to fall away. Like leaves. Pound by pound. It was like this mother I carried around in me. I gave birth to her when she died. I pushed her out. I get scared. She could come back.

You know, Eve, I like this group. Maybe I could share again sometime. Okay?

Diet plan: kill my mother. It would definitely be as popular as South Beach, no carbs and really good exercise. Just kidding. Kind of. I don't want to kill my mother. I want to stop freaking her out, scaring her off. Maybe she could tolerate who I was if there was less of me. The Vagina Monologues *is about to open here, in the capital of lipo, Rio. I end up on the beach of Ipanema. Every woman looks like she was born tan, flat, with a tattoo that serves as a bikini. I am flabby and suburban and white.*

The producers are courting this supermodel. They ask me to go and meet with her. I think I'm going to a photo shoot and I end up in the middle of her surgery. I watch as a masked doctor rams and sucks, rams and sucks, rams and sucks a steel rod into her thighs and her fat pours into a bucket by the side of the bed.

I have never felt so attached to my stomach.

Tiffany

A THIRTY-FIVE-YEAR-OLD MODEL

Come in, Eve. It's fine. Don't worry. I do this all the time; I'm just a little sore. I've heard people say that they've been changed by someone, but they don't mean literally. My surgeon literally changed me with his hands, with his instruments, with his vision. He removed some things and added others. I'm not anything like the person I was six years ago.

I went to him originally because another doctor had really botched my breast implants. My left breast was deflated and looked really odd, like all the life from it was gone. Ham, that's my surgeon's name, well, because he looks like one—bald, fat, short, Ham. He was horrified at the mess the previous doctor had made, and he actually seemed a little tiffed with me. Like I wasn't committed to making this the bestest, goodest body it could be. That is Ham's mission. I mean, that's what he does.

I'm not sure that I ever had the confidence to even imagine being perfect. I mean, I liked having a few extra glasses of wine, or sleeping till noon, or letting my hair go unwashed a few extra days.

Ham really changed all that. He's very strict. After I woke up from my first surgery, he was there standing over me. He was very excited. He had taken a life-size photograph of my entire body naked. It felt a bit invasive. I mean, I am shy and I didn't really know him. There were corrective red marks all over my body like the kind you got on your spelling mistakes in seventh grade. I was still groggy, but Ham's enthusiasm got through. "Your body is a map," he said. "These red marks are designated beauty capitals that need renovation and work." That was six years ago and today I am a Ham creation. I've had lipo on my stomach, butt, and thighs. He's gone back in with each at least three times to get it right, well, four, he did my thighs again today. I have newer Soya breast implants that do not harden and feel kinder to the touch. That was for Ham. We started dating after he made my tits softer. They really turned him on. He was doing the checkup exam about a month after the surgery. He was feeling my breasts all doctorly. Then something changed. It just got different. Before I knew it, Ham had climbed up on top of the examining table and we were doing it. I think how wonderful it must be for him to actually make love to what he's created. It must be very satisfying, and it's good, Eve. Twice during sex he's discovered areas with his fingers and tongue that needed more work.

Ham says it's good I'm only thirty-five so all this will last for a while. It was after he did my lips that he proposed to me. I think it was my little pouty pouch that made me irresistible. We're married now, two years. Some people have cafés or bookshops:

we've got my body. It's our small business. It's a joke Ham and I make, but we're doing pretty well. I've won several major beauty contests and I've booked lots of commercials and magazines.

But more importantly, my body is a great advertisement for Ham. He's gotten so much new business.

Ham is devoted to me. He is always so kind, particularly when I first wake up from surgery. He knows how much it terrifies me. Ever since the "cardiac episode." It was during my second breast implant that my heart kind of stopped. I felt so bad for Ham. He had just finished this beautiful work on my breasts and he was going to have to ruin it by compressing my chest. Fortunately he waited and my heart started on its own.

Sometimes I worry what will happen when he runs out of parts of me to change. Or that he'll be intimidated by the perfection of his own creation. But what worries me most is that he'll just get finished and lose interest. That's why I've secretly never given up ice cream.

I do not particularly like ice cream—the carbs, the dairy, the fat, my father. He was the president for many years of Popsicle Industries. Can you imagine? Mr. Food. This is true. I am not making it up. His proudest achievements were the Fudgsicle, the Cream-sicle (you remember, orange on the outside, vanilla in), and one that he actually invented in the sixties. It was called some faux-hippie name like Swingsicle. We were taught from a young age to distinguish the real from the fake, the real being real sugar, real fat, real vanilla, real processed. Borden's and Schrafft's were real—good upper-middle-class ice cream. Good Humor was cheap. We were not allowed to eat it. So you can imagine how much I coveted the toasted-almond Good Humor that we could get outside our school. I bought it every opportunity I could until I bit into it once and found something green, disturbingly green, and was sure I would die from it and when they traced the origins of my death, my father would learn that I had lied, I had betrayed him, and he was right after all. Good Humor was bad. I loved my father. I was desperate to please my father. I was taken by my father. I was invaded by my father. Then I was beaten by my father. I moved away from my body in order to get away from my father. I was bad. Very bad. I didn't listen. I talked back. I stole sunglasses, earrings, and fruity-flavored lip gloss. I would give them away at school to buy my popularity. It didn't work. I was wildly promiscuous, with a compulsive exhibitionist streak. In other words, I couldn't stop taking off my clothes. I did heroin the night before my SATs. Did you know you can get 200 points just for signing your name? Now I'm middle-aged bad. I talk with my mouth full and get food on my clothes. I sit right on public toilet seats and I don't wear underwear when I try on bathing suits. I secretly wish crying babies would go away. I'm too angry to be good. I don't have the goods to be good. So I'll just be bad. I'll go for it. I'll celebrate it. I'll flaunt it. Have belly, will show it. Watch me.

Dana

AN EARLY-TWENTIES BODY ARTIST

Eve, there's something about metal in flesh. It's so visual. I don't know anyone who hasn't seen the steel bars in my nipples. Do you want to see, Eve? It might give you some ideas . . . about what you want. I like wearing a tight T-shirt, like today. People are like, "Hey, what's going on in there?" Or when I'm at work doing the corporate thing, I'm the only one who knows. It's naughty. My nipples are in there whispering, "I'm not the good girl like you think."

I'm gonna start you off with a basic silver plug for your belly button. No, a semiprecious stud. That's hot for your age. See. You'll be back. You'll be piercing everything, it's addictive. Some people see my tits and are really disgusted. Some people are in awe. Some people get seriously turned on. I like it all. Come on, don't you want to see?

Listen, if you're too feminine, you're not really a dyke. Once you say you're a lesbian you have to have always been a lesbian and promise to be a lesbian forever. Can't really waver. Dykes won't trust you if they don't feel like you're in it for the long haul.

After I pierced my tits they became much more alive. I just have to wiggle the steel bar and my nipples just pop up. We're going to wake your belly up today, give her a second life.

I had my nipples pierced by a big hairy bearded lesbian. It was really hot. I kind of knew she was getting off with the power, with hurting me. Made it sexy. It was completely erotic. I gave her total control. Are you ready to start?

Don't worry, your body probably won't register it

as pain. It's more like a sharp, concentrated feeling. This is the sexy part right now, the preparation. Your heart's pounding. You're about to turn your will over to me.

My piercings are about evolving multiple definitions of myself as a woman, as a lesbian. These metal bars break open the way for me to be complicated. No one is going to tell me who the fuck I am.

Listen, when people see your pierced belly, they'll be disgusted or excited, but I promise you, either way they're gonna take your stomach seriously.

I run away.

Turns out I'm a little too old for "Fuck you."

I really don't want people to take my stomach seri-ously. I just want someone to take it. I read about a laser rejuvenation center and I picture light beams frying my fat. Where else would it be but Hollywood?

If America is the nuclear reactor pumping out the per-
fected standardized female image, Hollywood's the
core. I crave a meltdown. In my rental car, I punch in
the address for the laser rejuvenation center in my
handy Never Lost system and I end up in a vulva
support group by mistake. Try as I might, I cannot
get away from vaginas. I performed The Vagina
Monologues *for six years. I said the word "vagina"*
"vagina" "vagina" "vagina" nearly a million times, I

thought I was home free. I had finally come to like my vagina. Until one day I realized the self-hatred had just crept up into my stomach. At the vaginal laser rejuvenation center, women come from all over the country to tighten their vaginas and make their not-so-symmetrical labia minora and majora look more like zippers. It's a wildly growing business.

I meet Carol in her third week of her vulva esteem group.

Carol

A FORTY-PLUS JEWISH WOMAN

FROM LOS ANGELES

To be honest, sex has always been a lot of work. Harry, my husband. He's older than me. Twenty years. Well, twenty plus. You know I spend a lot of time with my hand, with my mouth . . . working, working to make Harry, well, harder, harder. But no matter how much I . . . he never really gets hard. Not hard hard. It's exhausting. Exhausting. Like eating

---

lobster, the mess—the cracking—the shell, the plastic bib, the little piece of meat inside the little lobster leg. Really, what do you end up with? I'm always starving afterwards. It was easier before. Well, not that much easier. But at one time he got hard enough to make the kids, if you know what I mean. Don't get me wrong. I'm not exactly pliant. I am forty. Well, forty plus. It's a little slippery after the babies, and Harry, well, he just can't get a grip. Listen, he was never the size of a . . . Never mind. I read about the procedure in *Cosmo*. I say to myself, Carol, Carol, there are laser beams now that can tighten your aging vagina. Utilize. So I go. The surgical center is right here in Beverly Hills. Well, close. We live in Brentwood.

It's a lovely center. Clean, well lit, marble everywhere. Actually it was a little cold with all the marble. I would think you might want something softer, something pashmina. But then again, it's not a clothing store. No. No, it's surgery. You feel secure with the marble. It indicates the surgeon's successful. And he was lovely—wonderful bedside manner. He spends all kinds of time with me, the doctor, Dr. Widener. Can you believe it? Dr. Widener, tightening. He shows me one of those plastic demonstration vaginas and begins to describe *Lalalalala*. Doctor, I don't really need to know the details, do I? You'll drug me. I'll wake up groggy. I'll be tighter. All I need to know. I decide not to tell Harry in advance. I'm gonna surprise him for his birthday. It's the big one. I tell him I'm going to Palm Springs. And I do, but after my surgery, with my sister-in-law, Shelly. Shelly brings me to the center. I think she's a little off. She asks me, "Carol, Carol, what will you do if Widener lasers you shut by accident?" I can't really figure out the logistics of this "accident" and then of course, I realize she's jealous. I don't know when she had sex the last time and I sense she's got a bit of a drafty port down there herself.

I don't know why, but I'm not even nervous. I just keep thinking about all the work, the work, the work and how it's going to be so much better and maybe, call me crazy, we can even focus a little on me and my sexual needs. I keep picturing myself clean, neat, tight. We'll start again, Harry and me, a whole new rediscovery process.

Okay. Cut to six weeks postsurgery. Walking, peeing. I don't think so. I kept making the dumbest excuses. I couldn't have sex with Harry. Actually I was nervous. To be honest, I felt down there and I couldn't find the hole. I was sure Harry wasn't going to find it, either. He was never exactly Christopher Columbus. So I decided to alert him in advance. I broke it to him on Sunday over brunch at the Ivy. He got very emotional. He really surprised me. I mean, he couldn't believe it. That I had had surgery and everything for him so he'd be happier and more excited. The last time I saw him like this was at Ethan's bar mitzvah.

Then we get home, it was like something changed in him. He got younger and more vital. He ripped off my clothes. I never saw Harry move like that. I didn't even touch him. No hands. No mouth. (*Moves her mouth*) He was just there. My Harry. Well, not my Harry. My new Super Harry. And then he, well, there was enough of him. He entered me. I have to confess it was very, very . . . painful. But I didn't let him know, the way you don't let them know the first time 'cause you don't want to alarm them and have them lose their erection and I was very tight and small, well, like a virgin, well, (*whispers*) like a baby, and I wasn't breathing 'cause it hurt so much and Harry was young, too, and hard, and then the tightness caused this friction, which made him harder, and it was painful, very, very, very painful. I was even crying a little. But I kept seeing the future, so I could bear the pain.

Now I'm exhausted in a whole new kind of way. Harry, always ready, always there—poised, set to go like a hunting dog. Nose in the air. He just has to think about my virginal vagina . . . and bingo. And he goes on and on. I say Harry, Harry. Harry, it's been three times today, dear. But he isn't listening. Sometimes I wonder whether I should have just closed the store altogether. Left a sign. GONE SHOPPING. BACK AFTER PRADA. I gave him something new like one of those Sharper Image watches and I know, when the novelty wears off—because, apparently the tightness never does—I know he's going to develop some finesse and subtlety. He's a teenage boy right now. He's got the hardness. But later, he'll adjust. It won't be such a big deal and then he'll be able to take some time for me.

When my partner rubs my stomach I want to vomit.
When he says, "I love your tummy," it feels obscene.
Recently, we were in bed, he told me his theory about
my belly—that it's this little hill that conceals the val-
ley of mystery and makes it much more exciting before
you get there. He says my tummy is my sexy, feminine
part. When it's soft, he knows I'm ready. He says,
Without your stomach I'd be stupping bone. While he
was saying all this, do you know what I was thinking?
Why didn't I pick someone with higher standards?
What is wrong with him?

I hate this ball. This ball is hard. Hardness is tough. Hard bounces off. Hardness is can't get in, can't get close. Hardness is invulnerable, is impervious. I'm trying to get hard, my partner is trying to get in. Talk about gender confusion.

I'm starving. Did I tell you, pretzels are now out. Turns out, they don't go with my blood type. Now, it's all about kale. Kale. What the fuck is kale? Where does it come from? Is there a kale bush somewhere? I pray daily for a parasite.

I'm in Italy to give a speech on war and women's

rights at a global women's summit. For the first three days I live on espresso macchiatos. I am totally insane. I can't stop talking, but I feel skinny. Then I get hungry. I try to write about the patriarchal paradigm of invasion, occupation, and domination but all I can think about is pasta. So I empower myself and eat three bowls. I am no longer opposed to preventive strikes. I am desperate for a belly annihilation, I find a gym. In Italy there is Puccini playing. Everyone is so relaxed and body casual. They aren't even trying and they are totally thin. Then there's my friend Nina, whose body I covet. She is close to fifty and looks twenty-eight. She's wildly successful and never breaks a sweat. (Starts sit-ups) *While I'm doing psychotic espresso sit-ups, do you know what she's doing? She's eating a bread-and-gelato sandwich.* (Stops mid sit-up)

Nina

AN ITALIAN WOMAN

Nina

Basta, Eve, *basta*. You look like a person about to
have a heart attack. I never knew you were such an
American.

Eve

Excuse me, Nina, some of us aren't so lucky as
you. How do you have such a perfect body?

Nina

Bella, bella. Things are not what they seem. You sure you want to know? Really? Okay, okay. Come, we'll have a cigarette. Let's pollute the gym. (*Lights a cigarette*) I was a very skinny girl. Flat like a countertop, sleek, smooth, everything slid off. And I was fast. Faster than any boy I ever met. I was the fastest. I was boss.

One day I was about to go swimming in this fantastic river and I look down and there is something growing there. Growing on my chest. I try to rub it off. With each inch I could feel the end of my freedom, the end of my life. I hated girls. They were so stupid. They didn't climb. They didn't live in nature. They didn't play in cemeteries. My titties grew so fast. Exploding on my chest. Suddenly Mommy, who never even noticed me, is all involved—she makes me get a bra. I hated it. All caught—the bra, Mommy all touching, tight, choking me. But the worst was the way the people looked at me. No one looked at my eyes anymore. Just these two huge events hanging on my chest. Like Christmas lights, growing and flashing there. I couldn't run so fast, I couldn't climb. I was suddenly a girl, I was no longer a friend. I was so unhappy. My life was over.

Then came Carlo, Mommy's lover. He was beautiful, oh so gorgeous, rich, intelligent. He was mythical, crazy, and so much fun. Mommy always had me on these strict schedules. With Carlo, I escaped everything. I remember the first time I met him. We were on his motorboat. I wanted to swim. Mommy said, "No, Nina, Nina, you do not have a bathing suit," which, by the way, I had stopped wearing because of my breasts. Carlo just picked me up in my clothes and threw me into the sea. It was fantastic. All adventure began with him. And he taught me things—like jazz. I learned how to listen to the currents and threads. He took me places. Museums and crazy Italian movies. But mainly, I felt Carlo could see inside me. He thought I was clever and funny.

One night—I was fourteen—Mommy went off to give birth to my brother, Franco. Carlo, *his* father, chose to stay home with me. We read our usual poetry and ate pizza. Then there were cozy little kisses.

It felt so good. Then he went further. I was paralyzed with fear and pleasure. No one ever touched me before. I had no way to say no. I learned about smell. I learned about wet. He licked me for hours. That night I discovered my breasts could give me pleasure. By being touched. Being licked. Being tortured. He said I was his and I was so happy to finally be owned and loved by him.

When Mommy came home, she was very sore and tired. She had had a terrible cesarean and she was ripped apart. I felt bad for Mommy. Gradually my breasts began to feel guilty, two huge chunks of frozen guilt on my chest. It didn't stop Carlo and me.

Mommy sensed something was happening. She was always angry with me. I blamed my terrible breasts. They were responsible for everything. Then one night as Carlo was giving my breasts this torturous pleasure, I felt so sick. I had a vision. I will get rid of them. Mommy always hated them so it was easy to get her to agree. For my sixteenth birthday, she gave me a present. It took twenty days. Ten days in the clinic. Ten days in Switzerland. I saw my feet again. My breasts were gone. *Basta.* I had a huge scar. I could play again as a boy. I was no longer a sexy woman everyone wants to fuck. I truly believed that being flat would protect me from Carlo and my desire. It didn't. It went on and on.

Isabella Rossellini

ACTOR; FORMER LANCÔME

SPOKESPERSON AND MODEL

Beauty.

The most beautiful woman in the room.

The most beautiful woman in the world.

Close your legs, Isabella.

Don't wear that, Isabella.

One more like that, Isabella.

Beauty—it says you want to make love.

I don't say no. It won't take long.

A few minutes, I'll get on with my life.

Like bathing my dogs.

They hold still for that moment when I soap
    and scrub.

They stand absolutely strangely still.

And then, when it's done

they shake

and they shake

and they're gone.

I hold still for him, like the dogs.

It doesn't occur to me that I'm a part of this.

No. It is my beauty, it is my beauty

that brings it on.

I wasn't meek in the photographs, no.

I knew how to express assertiveness.

I knew the glamour of strong women

who did what they wanted to do.

Like Kahlo, Magnani, like Callas.

I could do that in the photographs.

The corporation never really wanted that.

They accepted it until I got stronger than
    the creme they were selling to make
    women better.
The creme is the star, they said, not Isabella
    Rossellini.
They sent me so many flowers on my
    fortieth birthday.
I knew I was dead.
They said, "Be grateful, Isabella.
Be grateful you lasted so long in the
    business."
I didn't say no.
I must have meant yes.
They asked me to take responsibility.
They said making a fuss would damage my
    career.
But they had already ended it.
I didn't speak up.
It didn't occur to me that
I was part of it.
No, it was my beauty, my beauty that
    brought it on.

So now, please, let me say it. Here.

I was forty.

I was at my best.

I knew who I was.

Women wanted that more than the

lipstick or eye shadow or creme.

They fired me

because I was strong.

They told me not to talk.

I am talking. I am talking.

Everywhere

Beware. We are everywhere. Most of us are over forty. In your hospitals and schools, your churches and restaurants. Smiling now. No wrinkles. No surprise. We are virginal. Fresh. We live in camouflage. I teach kindergarten and your children like me better. They think I'm kinder and more fun. I work on Wall Street and when you interrupt me with bad ideas you can no longer tell how dumb I think you are. I work in Washington and you told me I could run 'cause I look pure, like someone's mother. We have poison in our foreheads, in our chins, like the head of a snake. One more false, humiliating move, you could activate the global posse.

Here are things that could do it: People who ask for my honest opinion and then call me a bitch when I give it. People who call it consensual. People who tell me to lighten up when I'm already fucking funny.

It's real. It's botulinum. It's in our bodies. A single gram could kill millions. My face could take out most of Manhattan. It gives new meaning to the notion of homeland security. Doesn't it? Who am I?

I am the Hillary Clinton who told Bill to fuck himself.

I'm the Princess Di who married that Muslim. I am the Margaret Thatcher who wears sexy bras. I am the Madeleine Albright who's proud to be a Jew.

Like Condi Rice, I am smiling at you. Not one

inch of this fucking rage leaks through. Here's the scary news—there are millions of us. We serve your tea. We hand out peanuts on your planes. We wipe your ass. We shred your documents. Call me a bitch. It doesn't matter. I like the name. Bitch Bitchbitch-bitch. I cooked three meals a day for twenty-two years and not one of you said "Thank you"!!!! I ironed your goddamn underwear. I sucked you off right before you gave your biggest speeches. I played those games in bed. I did, I called it Mr. Winkie. It's easier now. I look so open, so refreshing, so enchant-ing, so brand-new. It's easier to slip through. They can't check this bag at customs. The doctor shoots me up every couple weeks. My face is numb, but I'm in-sane in here.

You wouldn't let me in the club. Like you, I wanted access to the world. I wanted to be great. It's just a little bit more interesting than being good. We get pricked and we bleed and we call them botox parties. It isn't Tupperware this time, baby. It's the post-menses, not-sorry-anymore, not-many-years-left, smiling-at-you army. We are blood sisters. We are lethal. We are growing in numbers. We do not scowl. We can't squint. We don't look mad. We look relaxed. Like we've just had a nap. Like we're back from vacation. You will be drawn to us. Watch your toes. Watch your dick. Watch your back. One bite. Beware.

So here's what I think I've learned so far: In order to be good, I've got to be a smiling psychopath, deprived of pretzels, deeply involved with a Nazi trainer, fortunately numb from the botulinum, white vanilla fat sucked out with rods, and my pussy tightened. I would be sucking, spending, scrubbing, shaving, pumping, pricking, piercing, perming, cutting, covering, lightening, tightening, ironing, lifting, hammering, flattening, waxing, whittling, starving, and ultimately vanishing.

I need to stop.
I need to breathe.
I need to be here.
I want to be able to do my work.
I really don't want to disappear.

Blessedly there is a trip planned to Africa to meet a woman, Leah, who isn't cutting or tightening anything or anyone. She is fighting to keep young girls intact. I find this seventy-four-year-old woman in a field in the Rift Valley eating her lunch. There is blue sky in every direction. Zebras darting on and off the dusty roads. Tall Masai women in red and covered in beads.

Leah and I sit and talk for hours and finally I get up the courage to ask, "Leah, do you like your body?"

Leah

A SEVENTY-FOUR-YEAR-OLD
AFRICAN MASAI WOMAN

Leah

Do I like my body? Do I like my body? My body.
My body. I love my body. God made this body. God
gave me this body. My body. My body. Oh goodness, I
love my body. My fingers, look at my fingers. I love
my fingernails, little crescent moons. My hands, my
hands, the way they flutter in the air and fall, they
lead right up to my arms—so strong—they carry

things along—I love my arms—and my legs, my legs are long, so long, Masai people, we are tall, I get there fast, my legs can wrap around a man and hold him there. My breasts . . . My breasts, well look at them, they're mine, my breasts still round and full and fine.

Eve

Leah, wait, I don't know how to do this. I want to feel like you. I want to love my body and stop hating my stomach.

Leah

What's wrong with it?

Eve

It's round. It used to be flat.

Leah

It's your stomach. It's meant to be seen.
Eve, look at that tree? Do you see that tree?
Now look at that tree. (*Points to another tree*) Do

you like that tree? Do you hate that tree 'cause it doesn't look like that tree?

Do you say that tree isn't pretty 'cause it doesn't look like that tree? We're all trees. You're a tree. I'm a tree. You've got to love your body, Eve. You've got to love your tree. Love your tree.

Love my tree. Turns out I'm a tree. Love my tree. I'm all tree. My partner's been worried, so he visits me in Africa. We spend the night in a hut in a netted bed in a safari park. The sound of wild hyenas in the dark. I'm all tree. I'm all naked dancing tree. I'm all tree inside me. I'm all . . .

Eve

Honey, do you love my tree?

Partner

Every leaf, babe.

Eve

Huh. I didn't see leaves.

Partner

Yes, leaves and a solid trunk.

Eve

Solid . . . trunk?

Partner

Yes, solid, sturdy, trunk.

Eve

Sturdy. There is nothing sexy about sturdy. Sturdy is like a brick house; sturdy is like a boulder.

Partner

No, no, no. Sturdy is here. Sturdy is present. Sturdy turns me on.

Eve

Trees are willowy. I was going for willowy.

Partner

But you're athletic, Eve, you're strong. Full.

Eve

Full. Are you saying I'm fat?

Partner

No, full like fit, like sturdy.

Eve

You just said I was fat.

Partner

I thought you were a tree, Eve. Trees aren't fat. I thought we were dealing with tree.

Eve

Tree is gone. You chopped down tree. Now I'm a broken shrub.

Partner

I didn't chop down tree. Tree was clearly never really here.

I am so sick of your stomach, your shrub, your

trunk, your stump, whatever it is. I can never get it right. I don't have an issue with your stomach. I have an issue with you. You're not here. I want a relationship with Eve. I am not going to compete with your stomach anymore.

My partner leaves the next day. Only his olive pits remain, and there are lots of them. Maybe the programming's just too deep. I'm bereft. I can't go home. I'm all alone.

I get lost in India. Beggars, missing limbs, purple silk saris blowing on the beach at sunset, sacred cows lying calmly in mad traffic, saffron and marigolds and spinning wheels, the dead exposed in daylight, their ashes floating on the river, bindis and henna and curry and lassis and birds and monsoon downpours. Something comes undone in me. Something lets loose. My heart, my stomach, my sorrow. The longing for a mother. The betrayal by my father. The desperation to receive my partner. This emptiness. The need to go further. The compulsion to be more and more. I am

*falling, falling. I panic. I eat nan. Lots of nan. Warm
fluffy nan. I medicate myself with nan. Just because
it's called nan doesn't mean it's not Satan.*

*I'm a tub. I am a tub of nan. I hide in layers and it's
really hot. Fat and afraid of everything, I go back to
the gym. I can't believe I'm in India and I'm at the
gym.* (The ball bounces at Eve and she kicks it back.)
*I'm on the treadmill. Four days later I look down on
the treadmill and it's stuck on random. I am walking
insanely to my end.*

*All around me Indian women in saris and Nikes
are giving me the evil eye.*

Priya

Excuse me, sweaty lady. This is our treadmill, you have been on it for four days, you have to share. You don't look very well. Maybe give another girl a go. Thank you. My best friend, Neeru, she calls me *jadhi*. *Jadhi* is fat. That's because I *am jadhi*. It was Neeru who got me to come to the Sunrise gym. I have been coming here ten years and guess what, I'm still *jadhi*. But now I'm fit, full of pep. Oh, it was Neeru who told me about the infamous treadmill. At first, I

---

thought it was some kind of pastry maker. She said no, you can travel on it, it will take a *jadhi* girl like you brand-new places, and it has. What can I tell you, the treadmill gets me really jazzed up. I bring my own Walkman because, as you can hear, sitar is not exactly a boucing treadmill beat. I like the artist formerly known as Prince. All right, Kavita, all right. Have a go. You don't have to be so aggressive. You know, Eve, some days there is real treadmill mania. Last week there was quite a rumpus. Kavita over there, she's like you, she spends hours on the treadmill, refused to get off. There was a queue of angry *jadhis* waiting and waiting. Finally one of the real *jadhis* who can't even touch her toes just had it and got on the treadmill with Kavita and starting walking, "I will walk with you," she said, "as far as the Howrah Bridge." They were holding on to each other for dear life. It was treadmill mania. Kavita is really out of control. She is very very skinny. It's because of Miss India becoming Miss Universe becoming Miss World—now all the young girls want to be Miss Skinny India World. But I heard that when

---

Miss India won the World she was very, very hungry. She was tired of roti and sprouts. This beauty pageant business is getting uglier every day. All the girls look like TB patients. When I was young, no one would consider marrying a skinny girl. Skinny girls come from starving families. Eve, look at me— without my *jadhi*, how could I hold my sari up? Read the *Kama Sutra*. Indian women are very, very curvy and voluptuous. I think I am very beautiful. I love my cheeks (*she squeezes her cheek*), my dimples, right here. Kumar, my husband, calls it the seed of my smile. He gets excited and just grabs me here sometimes. Kumar was worried when I first started at the gym. He said "Priya, Priya, your *jadhi* is my personal country. I know the contours and landmarks. If you were to lose your *jadhi*, I would be a sorry refugee." Not to worry, Kumar. Not to worry. An ideal body? No such thing, Eve. There is no joy in perfection. Only in striving to be perfect. If you're perfect, you might as well be dead. Well no, I take it back. I *am* perfect. Perfectly *jadhi*.

The next day my prayers are answered. I get a parasite. I am sick, really sick. I should be thrilled. My stomach is becoming flat. Why won't it go away. I'm delirious and sweaty and in the dark. It feels too familiar.

Priya, my friend, calls a healer.

Lakshmi

Baba, where are you sick? (*Eve points to stomach*)

This happens in India. We call it Delhi belly. Does it burn?

Eve

Yes.

Lakshmi

Are there cramps?

Eve

Yes. I want it to go away.

Lakshmi

It will, Baba. These things take about a week or so. I brought you some medicine.

Eve

No. It's been here my whole life.

Lakshmi

Oh.

May I feel it?

Eve

I don't know.

Lakshmi

What are you afraid of?

Eve

Your touch.

Lakshmi

And what will happen when I touch you?

Eve

I don't know.

I will melt and disappear.

Lakshmi

And your stomach?

Eve

It will live on.

Lakshmi

Oh, it's very powerful, your stomach.

Baba, Baba, let me put my hands on it.

Eve

Okay. I guess. Go on.

(*Lakshmi unwraps her sari and puts her hands on Eve's belly.*)

Lakshmi

Stomach. It's where we connect to our mothers. Belly to belly button.

Eve

I just wanted to be enough, that's all.

I just wanted to be enough.

(*Beat*)

Lakshmi holds me in her *jadhi* arms.

She smells like jasmine and sandalwood.

Lakshmi

Eve, have you had a chance to see India?

Eve

Only the gym.

Lakshmi

That is not India. That is not our country.

I think you only know one country—a little country, your body with a population of one. You spend all your time fixing and renovating it. You're missing the rest of the world. You need to look up, Eve. You need to look out. (*Pause*) Oh, there you are. *Namaste.* Welcome, Eve. Welcome.

*Months later, I am in Afghanistan, back at work, in-
terviewing women who have barely survived under the
Taliban. All their rights have been undone. They live
in dust. I spend days listening to women who have been
beaten, trampled, who witnessed their husbands being
shot. I'm not sure whether it's because of my own his-
tory, or what, but I can't stop thinking about one particular story I heard about two young women who
were beaten severely for eating ice cream. I try to*

imagine how not eating ice cream is fostering virtue or preventing vice. I am trying to see my father as a pornographer, or an arms dealer or a pimp, making vanilla ice cream.

After I've brought it up about a hundred times, my host, Sunita, a patient revolutionary woman, says: "Eve, we have a special treat for you. We're going to take you to the secret ice cream–eating place for women. If we get caught," she says, "it could mean a flogging or even an execution. It depends what kind of mood the Taliban are in today." My heart is pounding.

We are quickly ushered into the memory of a restaurant. There is a room in the back. Four white sheets are pulled around us like walls. We sit. The restaurant owners are nervous. We wait.

The bowls of vanilla ice cream arrive. Sunita lifts up her burqa, keeps it cautiously and securely on her head like a wedding veil. She stares longingly at the bowl. She waits for me. As the Taliban circle the bazaar in their Toyota pickup trucks, the ice cream is no longer my enemy. Sunita is risking her life for this pleasure. She is sharing it with me. Finally, my being

fat is clearly less important than being free. I eat the
ice cream.

Eve eats the ice cream

> Sweet vanilla illegal melting into me.
> I eat the ice cream for the women in Kabul
>   and Kandahar and Mazar-e Sharif.
> I eat for Bernice,
> the body outlaw,
> who went chunky-dunking in the pool,
> making huge waves in the moonlight.
> She said, "I'm fat, so?"
> I eat for her.
> I eat for Priya
> on the treadmill at the Sunrise Gym,
> who loved her *jadhi*
> because it held her sari up.
> I eat for my Moscow translator,
> who told me she thought cellulite
> was anticommunist
> and she loved her pure Russian fat.

I eat for Helen Gurley Brown

that she will let herself be.

I eat for Nina and her lost breasts.

I eat for Carmen and her dreaded spread.

I eat with Sunita

there in the back of the Afghan restaurant.

I eat and swallow it down.

To keep the pleasure,

to keep the future alive,

I eat for all of them.

I eat for my partner

that I may choose to be open rather than

    hard.

I eat for my mother.

I eat for me.

Soft belly,

merciful belly,

receive, please.

Let the fat sweet sugary wet

enter and encompass me.

Let me not be afraid of my fullness,

let me not be afraid to be seen.

Maybe being good isn't about getting rid of
    anything.
Maybe good has to do with living in the
    mess
in the moment
in the ice cream
in the frailty
in the failures
in the flaws.
Maybe what I tried to get rid of is the
goodest part of me.
Think Passion.
Think Fat.
Think Age.
Think Round.
Maybe good is about developing the capacity
to live fully inside everything.
Our body is our country,
the only city,
the only village,
the only every
we will ever know.

Rome, Kabul, San Francisco, Los Angeles,
    Mumbai, Puerto Rico, Nairobi, New
    York

Our body is the carrier of the stories
of the world
of the earth
of the mother.
Our body is the mother.
Our body came from Mother.
Our body is our home.
We are crying here.
We are found.
We are women.
We are too much.
We are empty.
We are full.
We live in a good body.
We live in the good body.
Good body
Good body
Good body.

Special Acknowledgments

I would like to particularly thank Peter Askin, Ileene Smith, Gary Sunshine, and Priya Parmar for their invaluable help with the words.

I would like to thank Harriet Leve, Matthew Rego, Michael Rego, Hank Unger, Allison Prouty, Kelly Gonda, Joy de Menil, Nancy Rose, George Lane, and Charlotte Sheedy for moving this play into the world.

The following have supported my show, my

---

heart, my body, and my being: ACT, Kevin Adams, Paula Allen, Caitlin Bell, Nicoletta Billi, Cathie Bishop, Rada Boric, Clint Boyd, Robert Brill, Helen Gurley Brown, Oliver Campbell-Calder, Myung Hee Cho, Harriet Clark, Diana de Vegh, Bob Fennell, Jerri Lynn Fields, Eileen Fisher, Jane Fonda, Elisa Guthertz, Wendall Harrington, Deborah Hecht, Susan Hilferty, Mellody Hobson, Heather Kitchen, Lisa Leguillou, Elizabeth Lesser, Cecile Lipworth, Colin Lively, Vernon McIntosh, Pat Mitchell, Tony Montenieri, Emma Myles, Sheila Nevins and HBO, Shael Norris, Hibaaq Osman, Sharon Ott, Pratibha Parmar, Carey Perloff, Richard Peterson, Johanna Pfaelzer, Arabella Powell, Carol Fox Presscott, Sil Reynolds, Kim Rosen, Isabella Rossellini, the Seattle Repertory Theatre, Rade Serbedzija, Barry Silver, David Stone, Susan Swan, Lenka Udovicki, Ulysses Theatre Company, David Van Tieghem, Laura Wagner, Katherine Wessling, Marion Woodman.

I would like to thank the women whose bodies I love and whose stories I hold, from Greece, Turkey, Italy, France, Germany, the United Kingdom, Bosnia,

Croatia, Macedonia, Bulgaria, Guatemala, Mexico, the United States, Brazil, Kenya, the Bahamas, South Africa, Kosovo, Puerto Rico, India, Pakistan, Russia, Palestine, Jordan, Egypt, Israel, Australia, Canada, the Philippines, Iran, Korea, and particularly Iraq and Afghanistan.

I would like to thank the women from RAWA for taking me to get ice cream in Jalalabad.

I would like to thank my beloved family: Dylan and Shiva and Coco McDermott; Chris, my mother; Laura, my sister; and my brother, Curtis.

And my partner, Ariel Orr Jordan, whose faith and love sustain and inspire me daily.

ABOUT THE AUTHOR

EVE ENSLER is an internationally acclaimed play-
wright whose previous works for the stage include
Floating Rhoda and the Glue Man, *The Depot, Ladies,
Lemonade, Necessary Targets,* and *The Vagina Monologues,* for which she received an Obie Award. Ensler is
the founder and artistic director of V-Day (www.vday.
org), the global movement to end violence against
women and girls that was inspired by *The Vagina
Monologues.* In seven years V-Day has raised more
than $25 million for grassroots groups around the
world. Eve Ensler lives in New York City.